BEARPORT BIOGRAPHIES

CAITLIN CLARK

RECORD-BREAKING BASKETBALL PLAYER

by Rachel Rose

BEARPORT
PUBLISHING

Minneapolis, Minnesota

Credits

Cover and title page, © Brian Spurlock/Icon Sportswire/ASSOCIATED PRESS; 4, © Jeffrey A. Camarati/Getty Images; 5, © USA TODAY Sports/Reuters; 6, © Julio Aguilar/Getty Images; 7, © ZUMA Press, Inc./Alamy Stock Photo; 9, © EnriquePSans/Alamy Stock Photo; 10, © Ken Wolter/Shutterstock; 11, © Mitchell Layton/Getty Images; 12, © Michael Reaves/Getty Images; 13, © Maddie Meyer/Getty Images; 14, © Greg Fiume/Getty Images; 15, © Matthew Holst/Getty Images; 16, © Michael Hickey/Getty Images; 17, © Ron Hoskins/Getty Images; 19, © Catalina Fragoso/Getty Images; 20, © Jason Mendez/Getty Images; 21, © Ron Hoskins/Getty Images; 22T, © Mitchell Layton/Getty Images; 22M, © Maddie Meyer/Getty Images; 22B, © Ron Hoskins/Getty Images.

Bearport Publishing Company Product Development Team

Publisher: Jen Jenson; Director of Product Development: Spencer Brinker; Editorial Director: Allison Juda; Editor: Cole Nelson; Editor: Tiana Tran; Production Editor: Naomi Reich; Art Director: Kim Jones; Designer: Kayla Eggert; Designer: Steve Scheluchin; Production Specialist: Owen Hamlin

Statement on Usage of Generative Artificial Intelligence

Bearport Publishing remains committed to publishing high-quality nonfiction books. Therefore, we restrict the use of generative AI to ensure accuracy of all text and visual components pertaining to a book's subject. See BearportPublishing.com for details.

Library of Congress Cataloging-in-Publication Data is available at www.loc.gov or upon request from the publisher.

ISBN: 979-8-89577-037-5 (hardcover)
ISBN: 979-8-89577-462-5 (paperback)
ISBN: 979-8-89577-154-9 (ebook)

For more information, write to Bearport Publishing, 3500 American Blvd W, Suite 150, Bloomington, MN 55431.

Contents

Player of the Year

Caitlin Clark was all smiles as she stepped up to accept her **award**. She was being honored as Naismith Player of the Year. This is one of the most important awards in college basketball. It was also Caitlin's second year in a row winning it!

John R. Wooden Women's Player of the Year award

2024 was a big year for Caitlin. She won many awards, including the John R. Wooden Women's Player of the Year.

The Naismith Player of the Year award is given to the top men and women's college basketball players every year.

Girl Power

Caitlin Elizabeth Clark was born on January 22, 2002, in Des Moines, Iowa. Growing up in an **athletic** family, Caitlin loved to play sports. She started playing basketball when she was five years old. However, there weren't many girls' leagues around at the time. So, her father signed her up to play on boys' basketball teams.

Caitlin also played soccer and golf as a kid. She still plays golf today!

Caitlin's father, Brent *(right)*, was her first basketball coach.

Caitlin soon became a very strong player. In one high school game in 2019, she scored 60 points for her team! That same year, Caitlin joined the U.S. Women's Under-19 team. They won the gold medal in the U19 World Cup **championship**. In 2021, Caitlin played for the women's youth team again and earned another gold medal!

When she graduated from high school in 2020, Caitlin was named Iowa Miss Basketball.

The U19 World Cup championship trophy

Record Breaker

When it was time for college, Caitlin chose to stay close to home. She attended the University of Iowa and played **point guard** for the Hawkeyes. Right away, Caitlin began breaking records. In her freshman year alone, she scored an average of 26.6 points per game—with 40 percent of her shots being 3-pointers!

The Carver-Hawkeye Arena is the home basketball court for the University of Iowa.

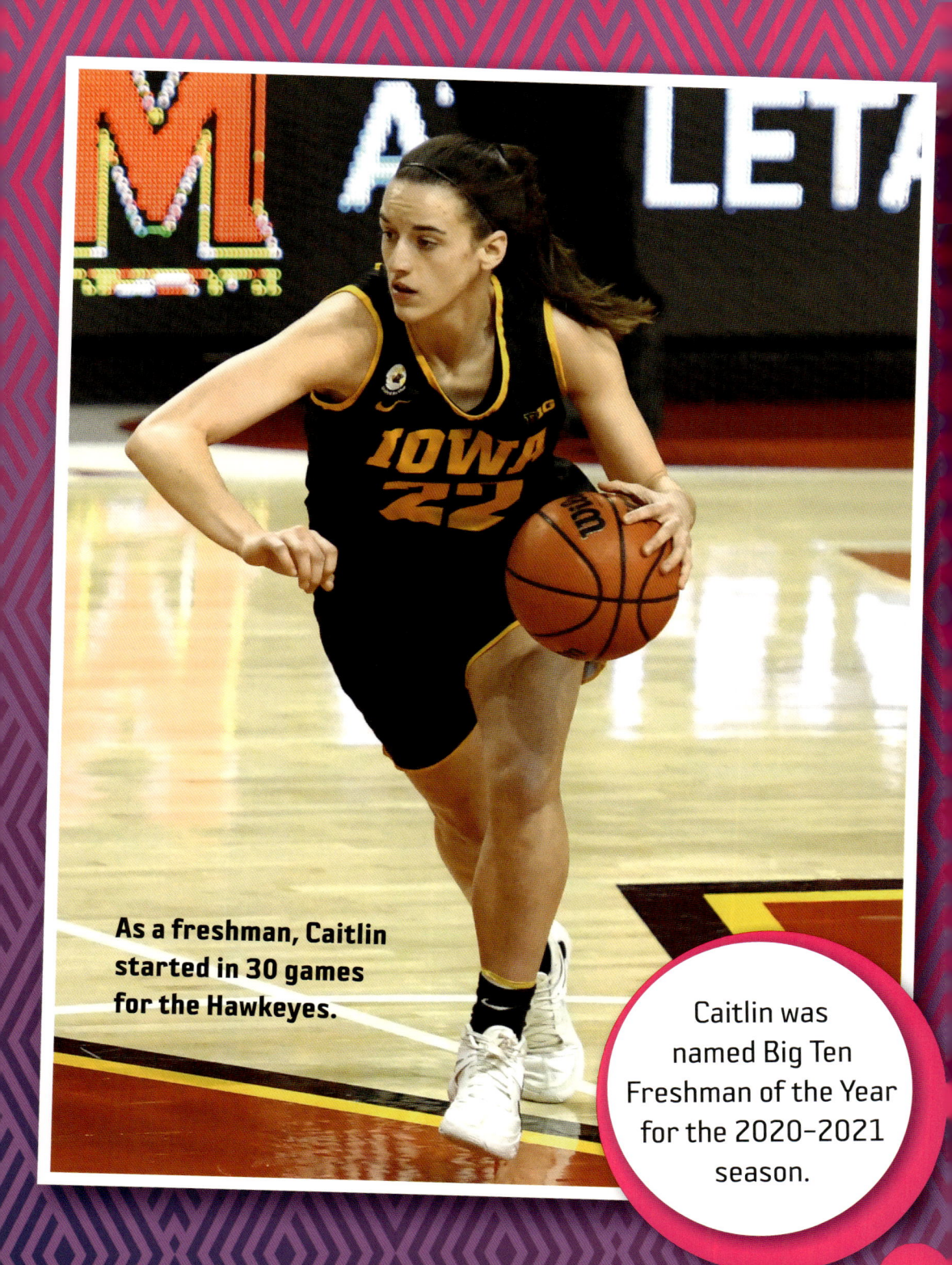

As a freshman, Caitlin started in 30 games for the Hawkeyes.

Caitlin was named Big Ten Freshman of the Year for the 2020–2021 season.

With every passing season, Caitlin's record-breaking skills on the court built **momentum** in the stands. During her final two years at Iowa, the games Caitlin played in drew record attendance. This peaked during the 2023 National Collegiate Athletic Association (NCAA) championship game between Iowa and Louisiana State University, which had 16 million viewers!

This increase in interest in women's basketball has been called the Caitlin Clark effect.

Caitlin scored 30 points in the 2023 championship game against LSU.

During her final year in college, Caitlin solidified her place in basketball history. On March 3, 2024, while the Hawkeyes were playing against The Ohio State University, Caitlin scored her 3,685th career point. This made her the NCAA's all-time leading scorer—in both men's and women's basketball! The Hawkeyes went on to win the game 93–83.

Caitlin became the Big Ten leader in **triple-doubles** during college.

Caitlin cheers after her victory against The Ohio State University.

Rookie of the Year

After her college success, Caitlin set her goals on something even bigger. She looked to the Women's National Basketball Association (WNBA). In 2024, Caitlin was selected by the Indiana Fever as the WNBA number one overall draft pick. She immediately made a name for herself, earning the title of the 2024 WNBA **Rookie** of the Year.

Caitlin is the only rookie in WNBA history to have scored a triple-double.

Caitlin received 66 out of 67 votes for Rookie of the Year.

Helping Others

While she was breaking records on the court, Caitlin also helped support others. In 2023, she started the Caitlin Clark **Foundation**. The organization's goal is to help improve the lives of youth and their communities through education, **nutrition**, and sports. Caitlin believes these are the building blocks for lasting health and happiness.

Caitlin's foundation has partnered with the Boys & Girls Clubs in Iowa as well as a local community food bank.

What's Next?

Throughout her career, Caitlin has worked hard and played even harder! She followed her dreams on and off the court, breaking records and making history along the way. Caitlin has changed how the world views women's basketball—and women's sports. Today, she continues to inspire new **generations** of strong girls. And Caitlin is only just getting started.

In 2024, Caitlin was named Athlete of the Year by *Time* magazine.

Caitlin's jersey number is 22, which is the day she was born, January 22, 2002.

Timeline

Here are some key dates in Caitlin's life.

2002
Born on January 22

2019
Wins gold in the Under-19 World Cup championship

2021
Named Big Ten Freshman of the Year

2023
Starts the Caitlin Clark Foundation

2023
Watched by 9.9 million TV viewers in NCAA championship

2024
Becomes NCAA's leading scorer

2024
Named WNBA's Rookie of the Year

Glossary

athletic active in sports

award a prize for being the best at something

championship a contest or final game of a series that decides which team will be the winner

foundation an organization that supports or gives money to worthwhile causes

generations groups of people born around the same time

momentum strength or force of something gained while in motion

nutrition the act of eating well so you can grow and be healthy

point guard the basketball player whose main jobs are to run plays and pass the ball to teammates who are in a position to score

rookie a player who is in their first year

triple-doubles when players have double-digit stats in at least three of the five major categories of points, rebounds, steals, assists, and blocked shots

Index

Read More

Goldstein, Margaret J. *Meet Caitlin Clark: Basketball Superstar (Sports VIPs)*. Minneapolis: Lerner Publications, 2025.

Jeffries, Corina. *Caitlin Clark (The Next GOAT)*. Buffalo, NY: PowerKids Press, 2025.

Learn More Online

1. Go to **FactSurfer.com** or scan the QR code below.
2. Enter "**Caitlin Clark**" into the search box.
3. Click on the cover of this book to see a list of websites.

About the Author

Rachel Rose lives in San Francisco. Her favorite books to write are about people who lead inspiring lives.